HABITAT
CONSERVATION

BY HARRIET BRUNDLE

PLANET EARTH **HELPERS**

BookLife
PUBLISHING

©2020
BookLife Publishing Ltd.
King's Lynn
Norfolk PE30 4LS

All rights reserved.
Printed in Malaysia.

A catalogue record for this
book is available from the
British Library.

ISBN: 978-1-78637-992-4

Written by:
Harriet Brundle

Edited by:
Emilie Dufresne

Designed by:
Jasmine Pointer

IMAGE CREDITS

CONTENTS

Words that look like **this** can be found in the glossary on page 24.

WHAT IS A HABITAT?

A habitat is a place where animals and plants live. There are lots of different habitats all around the planet. Habitats include forests, oceans and deserts.

For animals to live in a habitat, they need food, a source of water, air, somewhere to shelter and somewhere they can safely raise their babies.

An animal's body is usually suited to its habitat.

Polar bears have thick fur for warmth.

ECOSYSTEMS

An ecosystem is all the living and non-living things within an area. All animals and the habitats in which they live are part of an ecosystem.

My friends and I are all part of an ecosystem.

The animals and plants within an ecosystem all need each other in order to survive. If one part is changed, it can affect everything within the ecosystem.

We all need each other, Su.

CONSERVATION

Conservation is when something is looked after and protected from harm or damage. It's very important to conserve habitats and ecosystems.

Many habitats and ecosystems are in danger all around the world. This means the plants and animals living in them are at risk, too. We need to make changes to conserve them.

HABITAT
DESTRUCTION

Habitat destruction is when lots of damage is done to a habitat. This damage can be caused by humans or **nature**.

We need to stop causing so much damage to habitats each year to help look after our planet.

Natural causes of habitat destruction can include fires, floods or **natural disasters**, such as a **tornado** or wildfire. These natural events can cause damage to habitats, sometimes on a very large scale.

Wildfires like this one can kill plants and animals.

Deforestation is a type of habitat destruction caused by humans. Large areas of rainforests and woodlands are being cut down every day to make room for homes, farms or land to grow food.

Humans cause a lot of **pollution**, which can damage many different habitats. For example, plastic dumped in the ocean is killing sea creatures and harming their habitat.

This coral is dying, so these fish will be left without a home.

ENDANGERED ANIMALS

Plants often die when a habitat or ecosystem is damaged.

When a habitat is damaged or destroyed completely, the animals living in it are affected. Some animals are forced to find new homes, while others may be killed.

When the numbers of a **species** left in the wild drops very low, the species is put into a **category** to show how **endangered** it is.

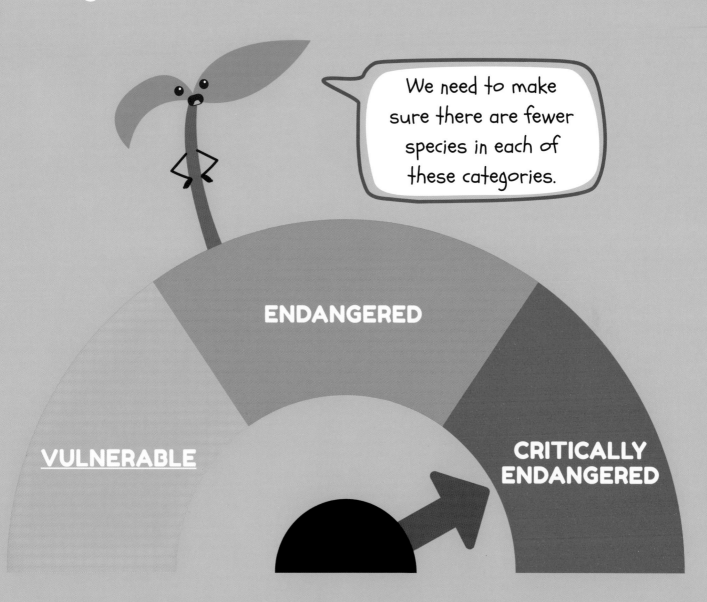

15

If a species has become critically endangered, it means there is a very high chance the whole species will become extinct in the wild.

More and more animals will become critically endangered if we do not help to conserve habitats all over the world.

BUILDING A HABITAT

Planting wildflowers and <u>saplings</u> like me will help to build a habitat that is full of life!

You can help to make a new habitat for the animals in your local area. Hedges, plants and trees make good homes for insects and other small animals.

Adding a pond, log pile or rock pile to your garden or local area can also make a great place for animals to make their home.

These areas are great for animals that like a dark or damp home.

CONSERVATION WORK

Lots of people around the world work hard to conserve habitats and ecosystems. These might be large groups, such as big charities, or small groups such as local schools.

> Conservation groups help to save little saplings like me from harm.

The WWF is a conservation group. They work with lots of different people to stop habitats from being damaged.

WHAT **CAN I DO** TO HELP?

Rubbish is a source of pollution which harms habitats. Try to reduce the amount you throw away, reuse items where possible and **recycle** when you can.

Tell your friends and family how important it is to look after us!

Why not plant some plants as well? Animals love visiting us.

Wow – this habitat is amazing!

Make an outside space a thriving ecosystem. You could also put up a birdfeeder in your garden or school playground.

23

GLOSSARY

CATEGORY	a group of things
DEFORESTATION	the cutting down and removal of trees in a forest
ENDANGERED	when a species of animal is at very high risk of going extinct in the wild
NATURAL DISASTERS	natural events, such as earthquakes or floods, that cause serious damage and loss of life
NATURE	everything in the world around us that was not made by humans
POLLUTION	harmful and poisonous things being added to an environment
RECYCLE	use again to make something else
SAPLINGS	very young trees
SPECIES	a group of very similar animals or plants
TORNADO	a storm with strong winds that swirl down from the clouds to the ground in a funnel shape
VULNERABLE	when a species is at high risk of going extinct in the wild

INDEX